MW01596498

Carrie Fitzgerald

The Needs of Children at the End-of-Life

A Case Synthesis

LAP LAMBERT Academic Publishing

Impressum/Imprint (nur für Deutschland/ only for Germany)

Bibliografische Information der Deutschen Nationalbibliothek: Die Deutsche Nationalbibliothek verzeichnet diese Publikation in der Deutschen Nationalbibliografie; detaillierte bibliografische Daten sind im Internet über http://dnb.d-nb.de abrufbar.

Alle in diesem Buch genannten Marken und Produktnamen unterliegen warenzeichen-, marken- oder patentrechtlichem Schutz bzw. sind Warenzeichen oder eingetragene Warenzeichen der jeweiligen Inhaber. Die Wiedergabe von Marken, Produktnamen, Gebrauchsnamen, Handelsnamen, Warenbezeichnungen u.s.w. in diesem Werk berechtigt auch ohne besondere Kennzeichnung nicht zu der Annahme, dass solche Namen im Sinne der Warenzeichen- und Markenschutzgesetzgebung als frei zu betrachten wären und daher von jedermann benutzt werden dürften.

Coverbild: www.ingimage.com

Verlag: LAP LAMBERT Academic Publishing AG & Co. KG
Dudweiler Landstr. 99, 66123 Saarbrücken, Deutschland
Telefon +49 681 3720-310, Telefax +49 681 3720-3109
Email: info@lap-publishing.com

Herstellung in Deutschland:
Schaltungsdienst Lange o.H.G., Berlin
Books on Demand GmbH, Norderstedt
Reha GmbH, Saarbrücken
Amazon Distribution GmbH, Leipzig
ISBN: 978-3-8433-5656-5

Imprint (only for USA, GB)

Bibliographic information published by the Deutsche Nationalbibliothek: The Deutsche Nationalbibliothek lists this publication in the Deutsche Nationalbibliografie; detailed bibliographic data are available in the Internet at http://dnb.d-nb.de.

Any brand names and product names mentioned in this book are subject to trademark, brand or patent protection and are trademarks or registered trademarks of their respective holders. The use of brand names, product names, common names, trade names, product descriptions etc. even without a particular marking in this works is in no way to be construed to mean that such names may be regarded as unrestricted in respect of trademark and brand protection legislation and could thus be used by anyone.

Cover image: www.ingimage.com

Publisher: LAP LAMBERT Academic Publishing AG & Co. KG
Dudweiler Landstr. 99, 66123 Saarbrücken, Germany
Phone +49 681 3720-310, Fax +49 681 3720-3109
Email: info@lap-publishing.com

Printed in the U.S.A.
Printed in the U.K. by (see last page)
ISBN: 978-3-8433-5656-5

Table of Contents

List of Tables   ii

Abstract   iii

Chapter 1: Introduction   2

Chapter 2: Review of the Literature   4

Chapter 3: Methods   20

Chapter 4: Results   26

Chapter 5: Discussion   35

References   41

Appendix A   66

List of Tables

Table 1 Overall Frequencies and Proportions of Needs   47

Table 2 Overall Frequencies and Proportions of Need Satisfaction   52

Table 3 Overall UNISCALE Frequencies and Percentages   57

Table 4 Proportion of Identified Needs Met   58

Table 5 Means and Proportions of Needs Identified & Met by Age   64

Table 6 Descriptive Statistics for Needs Identified, Needs Met, and Proportion Met   65

    by Cluster

Abstract

Evaluation of the unique needs of children with complex chronic health conditions and their families has captured the attention of researchers and clinicians. As medical research continues to improve treatments and survival rates for many children with life-threatening illnesses, the need for ongoing assessment of children's needs is essential to understanding these needs and maximizing quality of life. A model of the needs of these children has recently been proposed (Donnelly, Huff, Lindsey, McMahon & Schumacher, 2005). The purpose of the present study is to examine the content validity of this model via a case synthesis. Case synthesis is a recently developed method akin to meta-analysis. 49 cases met the eligibility criteria established for this study. The results of the study suggest that the model is relatively comprehensive, but six additional needs were identified. In addition, a strong positive correlation was observed between the proportion of needs met and an overall rating of the child's quality of life. The results of the study will help to refine the content validity of the model and suggest future directions for research on the needs of this population.

CHAPTER 1

NATURE OF THE STUDY

Introduction

In recent years, parents, healthcare professionals, and researchers have grown increasingly concerned about the specific needs of children with serious health conditions. Oftentimes, children are viewed merely as smaller versions of their adult counterparts. This could not be more untrue. Children are unique beings with their own set of needs, wants, motivations, and understandings of the world around them. While sick children share the same basic needs as their non-ill peers, they "may have a large variety of health needs over and above those of their healthy peers" (Perrin et al., 2000, p. 277). Because physical and psychosocial needs are complex and numerous among these children, meeting these needs is a difficult process for all involved in the child's care (Perrin et al., 2000).

At the forefront of this list of additional health needs are the physical needs of ill children, such as pain relief, nutrition, and disease treatment. These needs are fundamentally important with regard to survival, and must be satisfied first and foremost (Joy, 2001). Higher-order needs such as love, self-esteem, self-realization, and spiritual needs are commonly overlooked, since the primary motivation of caretakers is symptom management and curative treatments. According to Perrin et al. (2000), however, "most research suggests close to double the prevalence of emotional, developmental, and educational difficulties among children with a chronic condition as compared with healthy children" (p.278).

Children that are enduring complex chronic illness may face end-of-life issues. When the focus of health care evolves from curative to palliative, preserving the child's quality of life is foremost. While difficult, this overt recognition of the transition from curative to comfort care is

1

often welcomed by ill children and their parents, who believe that the child's quality of life is of primary importance. This recognition contrasts with the reluctance of many physicians to abandon curative strategies as well as cost conscious health management organizations and has led to debate over whether palliative care, and more specifically hospice care, is appropriate for pediatric populations. While the formation of pediatric palliative care programs has grown in recent years, healthcare professionals have not been able to rely on any type of standardized, comprehensive needs assessment techniques in their design and evaluation of their program's ability to effectively meet the needs of ill children and their families. The extant research, while a step in the right direction, evidences a general lack of accurate and inclusive understanding of the needs of seriously ill children and their families.

In 2003, Donnelly, Huff, Lindsey and Schumacher reported the results of an Internet-based demonstration project aimed at creating an empirically based model of the needs of children with life limiting illness. Through multidimensional scaling and cluster analysis, 74 unique needs were identified and sorted into seven domains (or clusters) which included: 1) Dignity and Respect, 2) Pain, 3) Psychosocial Issues, 4) Family Oriented Care 5) Medical Care Access & Quality 6) Spirituality and 7) Decision Making. To date, the list developed by Donnelly, Huff, Lindsey and Schumacher (2003) is the only empirically based model of needs from which healthcare professionals and healthcare educators have to draw upon. The goal of the present study is to examine the correspondence of this list to the patterns of needs evident in the many case studies written about this population.

Statement of the Problem

The illness of a child brings with it numerous changes for the child, his/her family, and significant others in the child's life. Activities of daily living become secondary, while

2

managing the child's illness is of primary importance. Leisure activities are likely to become obsolete. Too often, the families become disconnected, as they desperately search for a cure for the child's illness. In order to counteract these problems healthcare professionals must be aware of the unique needs of the child.

Clearly, a thorough understanding the needs of seriously ill children and their families is necessary if these needs are to be satisfied. Though recent research has made small strides in identifying these needs, healthcare professionals have not been able to rely on a comprehensive model of needs that would tailor treatment to each child's specific needs. Few studies speak to the needs of seriously ill children and their families, and the studies that do address these needs have serious limitations due to poor psychometrics, validity questions, and inconsistency. Pediatric palliative care programs, while relatively young, attempt to aim to meet these needs through a team-oriented approach. This team commonly includes physicians, nurses, psychological support staff, child life specialists, and the child's parents; depending on the child's age, he/she is also given varying amounts of autonomy with regard to medical decision-making. Because the field is hampered by a lack of research and diagnostic tools, there is a need for validation of the current needs model proposed by Donnelly, Huff, Lindsey and Schumacher (2003).

Importance of Study

One reason for this gap in the research is the difficulty of conducting studies of dying children and their families. However, case studies are a non-invasive method for validating the needs model. The case-synthesis method allows for a systematic assessment of the information contained in each of the relevant cases and will, in our opinion, contribute to the understanding of the needs of seriously ill children and their families. This study attempts to inform hospice and palliative care professionals of the typical needs reported by sick children and their families; once informed of these needs, healthcare professionals are better able to anticipate needs of children and families in their care, and can then meet them on a more consistent basis.

CHAPTER 2

REVIEW OF THE LITERATURE

A review of the literature was conducted to give an overview of the important concepts related to pediatric illness needs and their relationship with quality of. Databases searched included *ERIC*, *Psychlit*, *PsychInfo*, and *Medline*. The literature search and subsequent review confirmed the existence of a gap in the literature. Although the body of literature on quality of life and the needs of seriously ill children has grown in recent years, little was found concerning the specific question of this study. The main areas considered relevant were needs – the needs of seriously ill children, in particular – and quality of life. For the purposes of methodological background, the literature on qualitative research, and more specifically, the case study approach, was also reviewed. Finally, an extensive search for case studies was conducted and is described fully in Chapter 3.

Human Needs

According to McHale and McHale (1979) "the assessment of human needs, even at the basic level, is a moving target...Individual needs vary considerably according to age, sex, activity, climate, and sociocultural values and situations" (p.15). Because needs and their satisfaction are conditioned culturally and socially, they exhibit varying interdependent relationships in different societies, cultures, and regions (McHale & McHale, 1979). Researchers have studied the role of humans' needs for many years, but there has been a lack of research on the particular needs of sick children and their families. Theoretically, there is an important link between need satisfaction and quality of life.

When discussing human needs many researchers, regardless of their field, immediately refer to Abraham Maslow's *Hierarchy of Needs*. Maslow, a humanistic psychologist, coined this term in 1954 to explain what motivates human behavior. According to his theory, the focus of all human behavior is the satisfaction of needs. Maslow classified human needs and arranged them in a hierarchical pattern that moves from basic needs at the bottom, to self-actualization at the top. Since its birth, it has been studied and utilized by psychologists, businesses, marketing professionals, and numerous others wishing to understand and manipulate human behavior (Joy, 2001).

Maslow's *Hierarchy of Needs* consists of five levels. Included on the first level—the most basic—are physical needs such as water, food, and shelter. Next in the hierarchy is the need for safety, followed by the need for love and acceptance on the third level. The need for self-esteem is on the fourth level, and the need for self-fulfillment, or self-actualization, is on the fifth. This need for self-realization, as it is sometimes called, encompasses an individual's need to accomplish all that is within one's potential (Joy, 2001). The need for self-actualization has been described as an ongoing process that may never end. Maslow believed that it was a very real possibility that some individuals may never satisfy all of their needs, especially the need for self-actualization (Kiel, 1999).

Although Maslow has provided a foundation for research on human needs, critics argue that his model is insufficient. When the model was first introduced, critics maintained that it was not scientific because it was not based on empirical research and lacked construct validity (Kiel, 1999). Because of changes in managerial and educational fields, many feel that Maslow's Hierarchy needs to be re-evaluated and/or reshaped. With its closed triangular shape, the model assumes that people move up the steps in an ascending manner (Joy, 2001). Critics today feel that this is not a valid representation, and advocate the need for a more liberal structure that displays the unending self-actualization process. Rather than re-invent a model of human needs, modern theorists suggest updating Maslow's Hierarchy to reflect the needs of today's society

(Kiel, 1999). While the general hypothesis remains an important and appropriate foundation, a

newer version might better represent human needs by presupposing various interpretations and

applications dependent upon the field in which it is being used. This might be accomplished

through the development of specific models of needs pertinent to different areas of study (e.g.,

management, health care, psychosocial, etc.), as well as the general hierarchical model proposed

by Maslow.

Needs and the World of Work

The fields that are most represented in the literature on human needs and satisfaction,

including Maslow's Hierarchy, are organizational and vocational psychology. Managers strive to

make their employees happy in an effort to increase production and loyalty. Marketing

professionals study human needs, and attempt to develop products and offer services that satisfy

the masses. The literature includes a multitude of research studies designed to understand these

processes (Zemke, 1998).

Human behavior in the workplace has been the focus of much of this research.

Beginning in the early 1950's, Maslow and his colleagues studied the lives of well-adjusted,

psychologically healthy people - a major deviation from behavioral and psychoanalytical

research of the time. This emphasis is what set Maslow apart from other humanistic

psychologists who were his contemporaries. Through his interest in the needs of "normal"

people, he became involved in the world of work. Maslow's observation of work habits and

general vocational conduct led to a series of journals and, ultimately, the publication of

Eupsychian Management in 1965.

Maslow invented the term "eupsychian" to describe an ideal society. He defined this society as a culture that would be created by one thousand self-actualizing people living apart from the rest of human-kind. Although the book was not widely read, it did have long-lasting effects on those who believed in and adopted Maslow's line of reasoning. The idea that if you treat employees better, their production will be better was an innovative assumption at the time, especially in the world of work. Maslow felt that good management, psychological health, creativity and organizational success were interconnected. Many of the postulations put forth in *Eupsychian Psychology* have influenced the way people are managed in the business world today (Zemke, 1998).

Much of the variance in job satisfaction is related to the degree to which needs are being met in the workplace (Loftquist & Dawis, 1984). Maslow's theory presumes that because basic needs are taken for granted in many societies, they are not generally considered to be occupational motivators. He believed that in order to improve production, managers must appeal to the higher-order needs of their employees by creating a peaceful and safe environment where workers' accomplishments are recognized and rewarded (Zemke, 1998).

Quality of Life

Maslow's Hierarchy has provided the framework for extensive research on needs and needs assessments. However, despite an obvious logical connection, until now there have been relatively few attempts to link need satisfaction with quality of life. Perhaps one reason for this has been the diversity in definitions of quality of life. Following World War II, Americans were introduced to the phrase "quality of life", which was used at that time to describe how good one's life was beyond simple material wealth (Wildrick, Parker-Fisher & Morales, 1996). Since then, the term quality of life has been defined in a variety of ways by different individuals and organizations. The field of quality of life research has a strong foundation in years of empirical research. There has also been considerable growth in methodology and application of findings that has led to a deeper understanding of quality of life as a whole.

Children's Health Needs

Some public health researchers feel that society has failed to adequately address the needs of young children and their families (Randolph, 1994). These researchers are striving for integrated action to increase the number of children and families that can access acceptable health services (Randolph, 1994).

The health needs of children and adults differ on many dimensions. Children are continuously developing, both physically and cognitively. Medical researchers have linked rapid brain growth and maturation, which take place during the very early years, to a child's capacity for learning. Environmental factors such as nurturing significantly influence an infant's ability to develop cognitively and adapt to the world around him/her. Self-esteem, trust, empathy, language acquisition, and social skills are all qualities that have their roots in the first three years of life (Randolph, 1994).

Throughout childhood, preventive and primary health care are essential to healthy development. Beginning with the mother's health during pregnancy, a child's health and development are based on a "continuum of healthy physical, emotional, cognitive and social growth" (Randolph, 1994, p. 26). Each child's growth and development is a unique and individual process dependent upon both biological and environmental factors.

Researchers from many fields have identified numerous inadequacies in children's health care (Parker & Logan, 2000). "Despite the nation's great wealth, unmet health needs remain prevalent among US children" (Newacheck, Hughes, Hung, Wong & Stoddard, 2000, p. 989).

9

Moreover, Newacheck et al. (2000) suggested that the prevalence of unmet needs may be on the rise. According to Randolph (1994), "reversing the negative impact of society's failure to address adequately the needs of families with young children" is of critical importance (p. 25).

Access to Health Care

Many of these unmet needs are the direct result of inaccessibility of care. For children, this lack of attention to and treatment of specific needs can severely affect health status and development in the near- and long-term. Untreated physical and psychosocial problems can result in conditions that last throughout an individual's life (Newacheck et al., 2000).

Schools today must be prepared to serve the needs of students who have health problems such as developmental disabilities, physical disabilities, psychosocial problems, and chronic health conditions. Unfortunately, the only health care professional some children have access to is their school nurse. School-based programs often become the primary mode of service for children with special health needs, especially those children who live in poverty. Underserved and vulnerable populations, such as the poor, have the greatest risk for developing complex problems as a result of their unmet health needs (Parker & Logan, 2000). Alarmingly, families with young children are often in the lowest socio-economic groups. In an effort to improve children's health services, researchers proposed a comprehensive, integrated system that addresses the following: responsible parenting, quality child-care, basic health and protection, and community support for children and their families (Randolph, 1994).

Complex Chronic Conditions

Definition of the needs of the population assumes that the population itself has been defined. A recently proposed concept, Complex Chronic Conditions (CCCs), appears to be a very practical and specific way to define the population. Feudtner, Hays, Haynes, Geyer, Neff and Koepsell (2001) classified illnesses into nine major categories which include cardiovascular, neuromuscular, malignancy, renal, respiratory, metabolic, gastrointestinal, hematologic/immunologic, and other congenital/genetic. Illnesses that fall into these one or more of these categories are labeled Complex Chronic Conditions (CCC's). These CCCs encompass an extensive array of *International Classification of Diseases, Ninth Revision (ICD-9)* codes.

Needs of Children with Serious Health Conditions

Researchers have grown increasingly concerned about the specific needs of children with chronic health conditions, such as the Complex Chronic Conditions mentioned above. As stated previously, children are not smaller versions of their adult counterparts. Although children who have a chronic health condition share the same basic needs as healthy children, they "may have a large variety of health needs over and above those of their healthy peers" (Perrin et al., 2000, p. 277). Health care professionals generally focus on the physical needs of ill children, such as pain relief, nutrition, and disease treatment. These needs are fundamentally important with regard to survival, and must be satisfied first and foremost (Joy, 2001). Higher-order needs such as love, self-esteem, self-realization, and spiritual needs are commonly overlooked, since the primary motivation of caretakers is symptom management and curative treatments.

"Most research suggests close to double the prevalence of emotional, developmental, and educational difficulties among children with a chronic condition as compared with healthy children" (Perrin et al., p. 278, 2000). Because physical and psychosocial needs are numerous among these children, meeting these needs is a difficult process for all involved in the child's care (Perrin et al., 2000).

Perrin et al. (2000), surveyed primary care physicians, mothers, and fathers separately about the number and types of services useful to chronically ill children and their families. The data were collected through a questionnaire that allowed each respondent to describe their own perception of the child's needs and the severity of the illness. The responses of those surveyed were then compared and analyzed. Although there was some degree of concordance among the needs listed by mothers, fathers, and physicians, doctors tended to rate the severity of the disease higher than parents did, though they identified fewer needs. Mothers and fathers were in agreement about the level of severity and their child's health needs. Although parents and physicians may identify different needs, some predictable clusters of children's and families' needs have emerged. These include: family support, information, finances, child care, social support, and professional services such as medical and psychological assistance (Perrin et al., 2000).

Mothers and fathers noted that many of their children's and families' needs were not being met sufficiently. The need for information was the need most frequently noted by parents as not being met adequately. Parents reported that they want to be informed at all stages of their child's illness about the disease, its treatment, and long-term implications. Medical information can be appreciated most by parents when given to them directly by the child's physician(s) and/or specialist(s). In addition, parents feel that their children's and families' medical needs would be better met if there was an integrated system of care supervised by the child's primary care physician (Perrin et al., 2000).

Results of this study indicated that health care professionals and parents often identify different needs for the chronically ill child. When similar needs were identified they were given varying importance ratings by doctors and parents. When parents and health care professionals agree on the particular needs of the child, long-term care plans that address the specific issues and concerns can be developed, resulting in parents increased contentment with the child's overall care. Parents reported that a collaborative, or family-centered, approach to care is likely to improve the process of care for the child (Perrin et al., 2000).

Because needs may account for much of the variance in quality of life in children, meeting the chronically ill child's particular needs is essential to maintaining quality of life. Enhancing quality of life in chronically ill children is a multifaceted endeavor. As a result, the already difficult balance of the unique and a collaborative roles of medical, therapeutic, and academic personnel are further complicated when dealing with a child who is suffering from a chronic health condition.

Interventions, Resources, and Support

"Supportive care services range broadly, from aggressive control of pain and effective symptom relief, to sensitive spiritual care and grief counseling, to respite and bereavement services for the family" (Feudtner et al., 2001, p. 889).

Medical interventions are generally given primary importance for a child who is not well. Sick children often undergo painful and intrusive medical procedures that affect their perceptions of their disease and their quality of life. Frequent visits to doctors' offices and/or admission to the hospital can significantly limit or decrease a child's quality of life. If quality of life is to be maximized, pain medications must be prescribed to allow these children to live in relative physical comfort. Programs and treatment protocols designed to minimize the time a child is away from home, and to maximize the use of the least intrusive and least painful procedures are beginning to surface. It is imperative that physicians inform the parents about the potential symptoms, complications, and prognosis the disease may give rise to so that parents are better able to explain the disease to their child and other family members. Also, the physician should be cautious when talking to the child about his/her disease. Children are likely to question their doctors and nurses, who must use discretion and give the child only the information he/she is seeking, on the child's terms, in a respectful way (Bluebond-Langner, 1978).

In addition to numerous medical interventions, therapeutic strategies are employed to address the psychosocial effects of the disease on the chronically ill child and his/her family. It is not unusual for medical staff and families to conceal the child's diagnosis in an attempt to protect the child. Despite these attempts, children usually learn about their illness in indirect ways. Non-verbal communication, eavesdropping, and conversations with other patients often make children aware of the seriousness of their disease, and in some cases, their imminent death. A host of emotions and cognitions arise from this knowledge, and the lack of open, honest discussion with significant people in their lives can increase a child's anxiety. Therapists and counselors can help a child explore and share his/her feelings, which in turn, may improve the child's comfort and adjustment.   In this effort, the therapist needs to understand the child's perceptions of and feelings about death (O'Halloran & Altmaier, 1996).

Since the child's illness affects every family member, family therapy is another intervention that may improve the child's quality of life by easing tensions, fears, and anxiety experienced by the child and his/her family members. Parents' lack of precise medical knowledge about their child's disease can elicit many negative emotions, which the child can very often sense. When their child is diagnosed with a life-threatening illness, parents report feeling devastation and many other difficult emotions. Family functioning, as a result, is impacted in many ways. When working with parents, the therapist must take time to counsel them about the benefits of open communication with their ill child and his/her siblings. Therapy

14

with the parents can include working on facilitating this open communication by providing help with both the content and process of conversations with their children (O'Halloran & Altmaier, 1996).

As stated previously, a child's illness touches the entire family. Research has shown that siblings of cancer patients, for example, are greatly affected by the illness. Healthy siblings of pediatric cancer patients have been called "the forgotten ones" because they very often feel left out and neglected by parents and other significant family members (Madan-Swain, Sexson, Brown & Ragab, 1993). Typically, the sick child becomes the parents' primary focus (Wallinga & Skeen, 1996). The family therapist can help siblings by validating their feelings, by providing support and individual attention, and by teaching them coping strategies. Sibling adaptation and adjustment are the focus of recent research on the functioning of families of chronically ill children (Madan-Swain et al., 1993).

More often than not, chronically ill children, as well as their siblings, wish to continue activities of daily life. Normality and routine are disrupted for these children in many ways, so they commonly seek stability in the school setting. Teachers, school counselors, school nurses, and administrators have opportunities to make the school experience as positive and as consistent as possible. School counselors, especially, can play an important role in enhancing the quality of life of chronically and terminally ill children and their siblings. Like the family therapist, the school counselor can facilitate open communication, provide emotional reassurance, and provide a safe environment for children to discuss their fears, guilt, and resentment. School counselors also play an integral role in helping the sick child's schoolmates and teachers understand and cope with the child's illness and the physical changes the child may undergo as a result of the disease and its treatment (Bessell, 2001).

Educators need certain knowledge and skills to be able to work effectively with chronically ill children. Research has shown that children that are suffering from life-threatening illnesses such as cancer are at higher risk for problems associated with psychosocial adjustment, including problems with self-esteem, anxiety, depression, poor social skills, goal-setting, school reintegration problems, and school phobia. The teacher has been indicated by children as "the key individual in creating a successful school environment" (Bessell, 2001, p.352). In-service training for teachers may aid them in better understanding the specific needs of sick children in their schools, and may also help them monitor cognitive functioning of these children more adequately. Teachers must be able to recognize subtle changes, be understanding, and be willing to make modifications for the ill child (Bessell, 2001).

In addition to providing some normalcy for the chronically ill child, attending school whenever possible may alleviate their feelings of isolation. A continuing focus on education is extremely important in spite of the devastating challenges the chronically ill child faces. Homebound instruction is often necessary, and must be implemented effectively if it is to continue to help the child feel connected to their peers and their school. In the past, sick children have noted that it is important for homebound teachers to remain aware of activities in the child's regular classroom if they are to maximize the benefits of the homebound experience. Having access to school-based materials, other than extras or leftover materials from the classroom, is also important. Supplemental tutoring can also help children to feel less academically inferior to their peers. Retention and placement in special education programs are not practical solutions for students who are functioning below grade level due to the effects of their disease and treatment, such as excessive absenteeism. Schools must be sensitive to the needs of seriously ill children, and creative about interventions to improve their quality of life (O'Halloran & Altmaier, 1996).

The Good Death

A child's death is rarely viewed as a positive experience by those who have not been exposed to such an event. When a child dies in a setting other than the home (such as a hospital) and/or experiences pain or anxiety, the death process is generally viewed negatively. Although the death of a child is devastating to a family, the situation can be improved with adequate preparation and appropriate support services. Care for dying children and their families must be tailored to individual circumstances and needs. Hospice and palliative care services often meet these unique and ever-changing needs by providing services such as home healthcare, which commonly involves pain relief in the form of oral and intravenous medication. Many children's deaths, however, have been described as "peaceful" when they take place at home, among loved ones, with minimal pain and anxiety and where the quality of the last days of the child's life were maximized appropriately.

Qualitative Inquiry and Research

According to Creswell (1998) qualitative research can be thought of metaphorically as "an intricate fabric composed of minute threads, many colors, different textures, and various blends of material" (p. 13). Through examination of the definitions of the various forms of qualitative research, several core elements have been identified. As a result of these multiple characteristics qualitative research is generally difficult, rigorous, and time-consuming. Undertaken in natural settings, the qualitative researcher takes on the roles of data collector and analytic inductive thinker who focuses on understanding participants and describing their observations in expressive and pervasive language (Creswell, 1998). Comprehensively defined, qualitative research is:

> "...an inquiry process of understanding based on distinct methodological traditions of inquiry that explore a social or human problem. The researcher builds a complex, holistic picture, analyzes words, reports detailed views of informants, and conducts the study in a natural setting" (Creswell, 1998, p. 15).

The "complex, holistic picture" that Creswell (1998, p. 15) mentions is in reference to a narrative that allows the reader to see the many dimensions of the problem being explored, and presents it in a fashion that displays the complexity of the issue being studied. Qualitative inquiry is different from quantitative inquiry in that it usually involves few cases and many variables; quantitative inquiry, in turn, focuses on few variables and many cases.

In choosing which method of inquiry to employ, researchers must evaluate the nature of the research question(s) and how it may best be answered. Electing to take the qualitative road assumes the researcher intends to explore a topic in which variables are not easily identified, the behavior of study participants or their population is not explained by theory. Qualitative approaches, in brief, are aimed at developing theory through detailed views of the topic being studied, which is generally accomplished, in part, through the study of individuals in their natural environment. To do so, the qualitative researcher often must gain access to the setting or field of study so as to gather inclusive material. Researchers may also choose to conduct a qualitative study if they have interest in writing in a literary style; because the writer/researcher is viewed as a participant (to varying extents) in the study, the first person tense is typically used to tell the story. Researchers are "active learner[s] who can tell the story from the participants' view rather than as an 'expert' who passes judgment on participants" (Creswell, 1998, p.18). For this and the multiple reasons listed above, audiences are generally receptive to reading qualitative research (Creswell, 1998).

Case Study Research

Jensen and Rodgers (2001) refer to case studies as possessing "intellectual gold that is absent from a large-sample study...because detailed information is reported about specific conditions that are present and critical events that occur" (p.237). The value of studying cases as a way to understand the experience of the participant(s) is unmatched by other approaches to research. Although critics of case studies feel that the attention to detail achieved in case study research produces only a "snapshot" that does not allow for generalizability, it is precisely this attention to detail that brings a rich understanding to the case (or entity) under investigation.

A case study approach is chosen when a researcher is interested in studying a case with clear boundaries. Contextual material relevant to the case is important in describing the setting for the case. Obtaining and relating an in-depth picture of the case is the ultimate goal of case study research (Jensen & Rodgers, 2001).

Although critics claim that case studies do not allow for widespread knowledge accumulation, case study research has, in recent years, been employed increasingly by investigators in various fields of inquiry (Jensen & Rodgers, 2001). The knowledge accumulation problem cited by critics of the case study approach can be solved through case synthesis. Because case studies are often done in clusters, "they can be considered retrospectively as a group for broader and richer analysis" (Jensen & Rodgers, 2001, p. 236). The cumulative analysis of a group of case studies will be termed *case-synthesis* for the purposes of this study. The goal of case synthesis is to inform and build on theory. Jensen and Rodgers (2001) emphasize the importance of "[raising] the level of analysis so that all of the evidence

19

from case studies is synthesized and considered cumulatively, providing a golden opportunity to evaluate change within units as well as between units over time" (p. 239). Thus, case-synthesis is a method of combining findings across both published research studies and unpublished case study evidence in an effort to produce cumulative and generalized results (Jensen & Rodgers, 2001).

CHAPTER 3

METHODS

Chapter Overview

This chapter focuses on the research design and method that were used in this study, including the research objectives, case identification procedures, instruments, and an overview of the data analyses.

Research Objectives

1) To identify the specific needs of children with complex chronic conditions in peer-reviewed published and non-peer reviewed published cases.

2) To examine the relationship of needs to child and family characteristics and outcomes.

3) To evaluate whether the needs identified in the cases have been met satisfactorily.

4) To assess the content validity of an empirically-based concept map of children's needs.

Overview of Study Context

A case-synthesis method was employed for this study. The case synthesis began with extensive searches of online databases to identify case studies. This included in-depth examination of peer-reviewed and non-peer reviewed case studies of seriously ill children. Studies chosen for inclusion in this project included those in which the subject (ill child) of the study was less than 19 years old and suffered from one of the Complex Chronic Conditions (Feudtner et al., 2001) and included information related to at least two different points in time.

In the one prior empirical attempt to develop a list of the needs of children with life limiting conditions, Donnelly, Huff, Lindsey, and Schumacher (2003) studied the importance and feasibility of meeting needs identified by experts in pediatric end-of-life care. This Internet-based needs assessment resulted in an empirically based concept map of the needs of children with life limiting illness. Through multidimensional scaling and cluster analysis 74 unique needs were identified and sorted into seven domains (or clusters) which included: 1) Pain 2) Decision Making 3) Medical System Access & Quality 4) Dignity & Respect 5) Family Oriented Care 6) Spiritual 7) Psychosocial. The case synthesis provides evidence of the degree to which the concept map has successfully identified the needs of this population as well as needs that are not represented in the map.

Cases

Participants were the seriously ill children represented in the cases studied. Most of the narratives found were written by a parent of the sick child, however a small number were written from the perspective of the child him/herself or a healthcare professional – usually a nurse or social worker. Cases relevant for this study included children ranging in age from less than one year of age to 18 years old. It was our goal to locate all of the available cases in order to achieve a comprehensive description of the shared experiences of childhood illness as they relate to needs (met and unmet) and quality of life.

Case Identification Procedures

An exhaustive search of the literature was done to ensure that we identified all relevant cases involving children with serious illness and their families. Systematic review of journals, books, and other sources (such as the Internet and personal contacts) was conducted in order to supplement electronic database searches. When a relevant case was located in a journal, a thorough review of that journal's table of contents for the five years preceding the relevant case publication was undertaken. In addition, the most recent two years' tables of contents of pediatricly-oriented journals were reviewed for relevant case studies. If one was located, the tables of contents for the five years preceding the case were conducted. Studies meeting inclusion criteria were coded using the Needs Assessment Survey (NAS).

Selection Criteria

The sample consisted of the extant body of cases; both peer-reviewed and non-peer-reviewed published case studies that focus on children with complex chronic conditions. Cases selected for inclusion in the study involve a child diagnosed with one or more of the complex chronic conditions (CCCs) identified by Feudtner, Hays, Haynes, Geyer, Neff and Thomas (2001). The CCCs have been categorized into the following areas: neuromuscular, cardiovascular, respiratory, renal, gastrointestinal, hematology and immunodeficiency, metabolic, other congenital or genetic defect, and malignancy. Requirements for inclusion were that the case be longitudinal (at least two time points described in the case), include sufficient information needed to code the child's needs, include both medical and non-medical components, and be written in English. *N-of-1* clinical trials that include an eligible child but focus on the evaluation of an intervention were excluded.

Instrument

The *Needs Assessment Survey* (NAS) was used to code information from each case included in the study. The NAS (Appendix A) was constructed from the concept map of 74 needs statements as they were originally identified by Donnelly, Huff, Lindsey, and Schumacher (2003). A research team of two doctoral students, the director of a pediatric palliative care program and a licensed psychologist collaborated in the development of this coding system.

23

Coding Procedures

Coding began with a general review of each case study. The cases were then read a second time for deeper understanding of the material.

The Child's Needs and Individual and Family Characteristics

Each case was evaluated for the presence or absence of each of the 74 specific needs. Each identified need was also coded as met or unmet. Dichotomous "yes" or "no" responses were used for each of the 74 statements. Once each needs item was rated, open-ended questions allowed for the identification and description of needs not represented in the list created in the Donnelly, Huff, Lindsey and Schumacher (2003) study. Once these previously unaccounted for needs were identified, they were evaluated as to whether or not they were met satisfactorily. Variables such as the child's age at diagnosis, age at case report, age at death (if applicable), gender, race, medical diagnosis, and school information were also noted on the coding form for each case.

Outcome Coding

In order to explore relationships between needs and outcomes, an overall quality of life rating was given for each case. Just as needs evident in the cases were coded via predetermined criteria, quality of life was assessed utilizing a modification of a well-known proxy scale for measuring Quality of Life (QoL) in a seriously ill population. Spitzer et al. (1981) developed several brief forms of QoL assessment for use by clinicians. The simplest of these indices is known as the UNISCALE. The scale was developed with input from cancer patients, their families and a variety of treatment professionals. The original scale asked the rater to mark within a box anchored at one end with "Lowest Quality" and at the other end as "Highest Quality". The low end anchor was described as: "someone completely dependent physically on others, seriously impaired mentally, unaware of surroundings and in a hopeless position" (p. 589). The high end anchor was described as: "someone physically and mentally independent, communicating well with others, able to do most of the things enjoyed, pulling own weight, with a hopeful yet realistic attitude" (p. 589). The rater's mark was then measured with a ruler to produce what they considered to be an ordinal level measure of QoL. The scale was shown to have good inter-rater reliability ($rho=. 69, p < .001$) as well as content and construct validity, including rank correlations above .60 for a variety of rater groups.

In the present study an adaptation of the UNISCALE measurement format was employed. Each case was coded on a scale of 1 to 10, with 1 representing the poorest quality of life and 10 representing the highest quality of life. The low end was anchored as follows: During the course of illness and treatment overall, the child experiences conditions such as: is comatose or rarely conscious; frequently disoriented, suffers from uncontrolled pain, has minimal social and emotional support, has minimal control over bodily functions, requires mechanical support to live, is unable to enjoy anything, has severe mood disturbance (anxiety, anger, depression, etc.), cries frequently, is unable to find meaning in life. The high end was anchored as follows: is alert and oriented, is physically comfortable with well controlled pain, has strong social and emotional support, is relatively independent with regard to mobility and other functioning, experiences positive affect frequently and negative affect within a range that is not overwhelming and prolonged, finds meaning in life.

Training of Coders and Reliability

Pilot testing of the coding procedure was undertaken with a subset of five randomly selected cases in order to provide validation for the NAS coding scheme. Agreement among our team of three researchers as to the presence or absence of each of the 74 needs was used to

25

ensure inter-rater reliability. The research team reviewed each item in each case in which disagreement in coding occurred. Discussion concluded when agreement was reached on the best coding for the item. The clarification in coding rules resulting from the discussion was incorporated into the coding procedures for the remaining cases. When the training cases were completed and procedures revised, the remaining cases were independently coded by two researchers. Consensus on any disagreement was obtained via discussion of all items in which the two coders initially disagree.

Analysis of Data

Research Objective 1) To identify the specific needs of children with complex chronic conditions in published and non-published cases. Frequencies for each of the 74 needs were computed. In addition, all needs identified in the cases that did not match one of the 74 needs were listed and summarized.

Research Objective 2) To examine the relationship of needs to child and family characteristics and outcomes. A t-test of the mean differences in total needs and needs met between the one vs. two parent families was conducted. Mean differences in total needs and needs met were also compared with the child's age and diagnosis. Correlations between the modified UNISCALE score and the number of needs identified, the number of needs met, and the proportion of needs met were examined.

Research Objective 3) To evaluate whether the needs identified in the cases have been met satisfactorily. The percentage of needs coded as met vs. unmet were calculated.

Research Objective 4) To assess the content validity of an empirical list of children's needs. This objective was evaluated by computing the total number of needs identified and met in each of the seven clusters.

CHAPTER 4

RESULTS

Research Objective 1

The first research objective aimed to identify the specific needs of children with complex chronic conditions in peer-reviewed published and non-peer reviewed published cases. Through systematic analysis of 49 cases, needs were assessed for the frequency and proportion of cases in which they were identified. Table 1 presents the overall frequencies and proportions of need identification. For ease of interpretation, items (needs), preceded by their NAS number, are presented in descending order of frequency of identification. Needs that were not originally included in the NAS, of which there are 6, are indicated by a plus sign (+). Table 2, which provides frequencies and respective proportions for needs satisfied, presents the information in the same manner.

Needs were identified with variable frequency, with an average number of needs per case of $M=18$, $SD=11.79$. The maximum number of needs identified was 48 and the minimum reported number was 1. Item 15, the most frequently identified item ($n=31$, Proportion $=.63$), represents "opportunities to be cared for by loving family". Additional highly identified needs were, item 20: "Fun" ($n=25$, Proportion=.51), item 43: "Love" ($n=25$, Proportion=.51), item 11: "Talk about their feelings and fears" ($n=23$, Proportion=.47), item 47: "Competent, pediatric-trained professional caregivers" ($n=23$, Proportion=.47), item 5: "Developmentally appropriate activities and information" ($n=22$, Proportion=.25), item 9: "To be clearly valued as an individual by having preferences solicited and acted upon to the extent possible" ($n=22$, Proportion=.25), item 28: "Effective pain management" ($n=22$, Proportion=.25), and item 59: "People, things, activities that make the child smile and laugh" ($n=22$, Proportion=.25).

28

Needs were met with variable frequency also, with the average number of needs met per case of $M=14$, $SD=10.89$. The highest number of needs met was 45, while the lowest number of needs met equaled zero. The most frequently satisfied need, item 15: "Opportunities to be cared for by loving family", was met in 55% of all cases ($n=27$). Other needs that were met with relatively high frequency included: item 20: "Fun" ($n=25$, Proportion=.51), item 43: "Love" ($n=24$, Proportion=.49), item 59: "People, things, activities that make the child smile" ($n=22$, Proportion=.45), and item 27: "Pleasant distractions from the situation" ($n=21$, Proportion=.43).

Three of the original needs failed to be met in any of the cases, including item 46: "Child life intervention in the home," item 57: "Access to a child-friendly website", and item 65: "Confidentiality". In addition, four of the six new needs identified were not satisfied: "Preparation for all symptoms/side effects of disease," "To be believed by healthcare professionals when telling them something is wrong," "A liaison between doctors, nurses, and the child," and "Consistent discipline." Information regarding the satisfaction of remaining needs is outlined in Table 2.

Of interest to the researchers was the fact that although item 47: "Competent pediatric-trained caregivers" was a frequently identified need ($n=23$, Proportion=.47), it was only met in 27% of the cases overall, and 57% of the cases in which it was identified. This may be due to the fact that parents and children often noted that caregivers seemed lack formal training in pediatrics, and at times seemed uncomfortable and even uncompromising when caring for ill children.

Research Objective 2

The second research objective aimed to examine the relationship of needs to child and family characteristics and outcomes. Of the 49 cases included in the study, it is notable that a mere 8 accessed palliative care services, while an additional 10 received hospice care, indicating the absence of comfort care in more than one-half of the population studied. Further, 29 of the 49 cases held sufficient information that facilitated a judgment regarding an overall UNISCALE score. The average UNISCALE score for children fell at 6.62 (SD=2.72). Most frequently occurring were UNISCALE scores of 8 (n=6) and 9 (n=6). Table 3 provides frequency and percentages for overall UNISCALE scores noted in the study.

In order to assess differential identification of needs by family structure, children were placed into one of three categories: children living with both parents, children living with just one parent, and children in "other" living situations. Of the 49 cases, 42 represented children living with both parents, 3 represented children living in one-parent families (mother only), and 4 represented other living situations. Children living with both parents, on average, identified 18.79 needs (SD=12.15), with an average needs met of 15.57 (SD=11.19) per child. Average proportion of needs met was .83 (SD=.21) while the mean UNISCALE was 6.96 (SD=2.49). Children living in one-parent families identified an average of 12.67 needs (SD=7.51), with a mean needs met of 10.33 (SD=6.03). The average proportion of identified needs that were met was .86 (SD=.19), while the mean UNISCALE score fell at 7.50 (SD=.71). The average number of needs identified for children living in situations other than one- or two-parent families was 13.25 (SD=10.05), while needs met averaged 6.00 (SD=5.60). The mean proportion of needs met per child in this subgroup was .56 (SD=.47), while the average UNISCALE score was 1.50 (SD=.71). Statistical significance of the differences reported was not tested because of the large disparity in cell sizes. However, the descriptive statistics point what may be a general pattern of end-of-life circumstances for children who are not living with parents or family. Both the proportion of needs met and the UNISCALE scores underline the importance of family support.

Mean differences in total needs and needs met were also compared by the child's gender, age, and diagnosis. Of the 49 cases included in the study, 26 of the children were males and 23 were females. Males (M=16.27, SD=11.52) and females (M=19.87, SD=12.04) experienced a similar number of needs (difference not significant, t, $_{47}$, = 1.069, p=.291). The number of needs met was also similar for males and females (M=13.77, SD=10.99; M=15.26, SD=10.96, respectively) and again the gender difference was not statistically significant (t, $_{47}$, =.475, p= .637). The mean proportion of needs met for males was .85 (SD=.21), while the mean proportion of needs met for females was .77 (SD=.27). This difference was not significant (t, $_{47}$, =.349, p=.728). Finally, the UNISCALE means for males and females were very close (M=6.29, SD=2.81; M=6.93, SD=2.69, respectively); again not significantly different (t, $_{27}$, =.634, p=.53).

Age was represented in six categories based on the time frame described in the case. The coding scheme for age attempted to accurately represent the time period reported in terms of age, but given the variability in the cases, produced categories that do not cleanly break in traditional ways such as infant, child and adolescent. The six age categories were, therefore: 1) "Infant Only", representing children ages birth through 1 year, 11 months (n=5); 2), "Child Only", representing children ages 2 years through 12 years 11 months (n=18); 3) "Teen/Adolescent Only", representing children ages 13 years through 18 years (n=7); 4) "Infant through Child", representing children of the age range birth through 12 years (n=11); 5) "Child through Teen/Adolescent, which represented children ranging in age from 3 years through 18 years (n=4); and 6) "Infant through Teen/Adolescent, representing children ranging in age from birth through age 18 years (n=3). One case did not specify the child's age, and was, therefore, labeled "unknown". The differences in these categories were examined descriptively, without significance tests, because of the overlap in the categories.

31

For children in the "Infant Only" category, the average number of needs identified was 9.2 (SD=12.83), while the average for needs met fell at 7.8 (SD=11.97). The proportion of needs met for infants was .78 (SD=.31), whereas the average UNISCALE score for this group was 4.50 (SD=4.95). Children in the "Child Only" category had an average of 20.06 (SD=12.47) needs, of which an average of 17.78 (SD=12.47) were satisfied. Children in this group had a proportion of .86 (SD=.18) of their needs met, and a mean UNISCALE rating of 7.11 (SD=2.67). The average number of needs identified for children in the "Teen/Adolescent Only" category was 20.29 (SD=10.73); the average number of needs met for this group was 18.57 (SD=9.54), while the average proportion of needs met was .93 (SD=.08). The average UNISCALE score for children in the "Teen/Adolescent Only" category was 6.50 (SD=2.38). Cases which represented children in the "Infant through Child" category had an average of 17.09 (SD=11.41) identified needs, with an average of 12.73 (SD=10.22) needs met, signifying an average proportion of .74 (SD=.28) needs satisfied, with an associated average UNISCALE score of 7.33 (SD=2.73). An average of 22.50 (SD=13.77) needs were identified for children in the "Child through Teen/Adolescent" category, while the average number of needs satisfied for children in this category was 12.00 (SD=2.45). The proportion of needs met fell at .55 (SD=.36), whereas the average UNISCALE score for this group of children was 5.50 (SD=3.12). Children in the "Infant through Teen/Adolescent" category had an average number of 11.33 (SD=5.13) needs, and an average of 5.33 (SD=3.21) needs met. The average proportion of needs met for the "Infant through Teen/Adolescent" group was .55 (SD=.36), with an average mean UNISCALE score of 6.33 (SD=3.22). Information regarding means and proportions by is presented in Table 5.

Children represented in the cases were also separated into two diagnostic categories: malignancy ($n=28$) and non-malignancy ($n=21$). The average number of needs identified for children in the non-malignancy group was 13.5 ($SD=8.61$), but was 23.95 for the children with malignancies, a difference that was statistically significant (t, 47, $=-3.40$, $p=.001$). The number of needs met was also quite different for the two diagnostic groups. The mean number of needs met for children with malignancies was 20.29 ($SD=11.92$) and for children with non-malignant diagnoses was 10.11 ($SD=7.71$). Again, the difference was statistically significant (t, 47, $=3.62$, $p=.001$). The average proportion of needs met was not statistically different, with the children in the malignancy group having an average of .86 of their needs met ($SD=.18$), while the children without malignancies appeared to have .78 of their overall needs met ($SD=.28$). Differences between the two diagnostic groups were also examined on the UNISCALE. The malignancy group received an average rating of 7.44 ($SD=2.33$) and the non-malignancy group had a mean UNISCALE score of 5.62 ($SD=2.90$). The UNISCALE difference was not significant (t, 27, $=1.87$, $p=.072$).

Pearson correlations between the overall UNISCALE score and the sum of needs identified, the sum of needs met, and proportion of needs met, were calculated and resulted in a non-significant relationship between the total number of needs met and total UNISCALE ($r=.13$, $p=.50$), a moderate, positive and significant relationship between the number of needs met and the total UNISCALE score ($r=.48$, $p=.008$), and strong, positive and significant relationship between the proportion of needs met and the overall UNISCALE score ($r=.75$, $p<.001$). Thus, it appears that the quality of a child's life in the final stage of an illness may be strongly related to meeting the child's specific needs, as the literature review had suggested.

Research Objective 3

The third research objective was to determine how well the needs that were identified in the cases were met. Table 4 gives a summary statistic for each need, which is the proportion of times the need was satisfied in relation to the number of times the need was identified. To allow ease of interpretation of the table, needs are listed in descending order of proportion of satisfaction. Each need is preceded by the original NAS number, or by a '+' sign where a new need is represented.

Nineteen needs were met with 100% satisfaction, indicating adequate support in these areas. Needs with perfect satisfaction were as follows: item 4: "Laughter for release," item 13: "Assessment of preferences and goals for social interaction and facilitation of those preferences and goals," item 17: "Translators if the child's first language is not English," item 18: "Being able to give home blood transfusions, especially platelets, so the child does not bleed out at home," item 20: "Fun," item 23: "Culturally-sensitive care," item 24: "To be reassured that he or she is important and will be remembered," item 26: "Prayers," item 27: "Pleasant distractions from the situation," item 38: "Ability for NP/MDs to make home visits," item 40: "The ability to transition in and out of the hospital as needed," item 44: "Peer support groups," item 50: "Networking with other children experiencing a similar illness, treatment, etc.," item 51: "The right to say no," item 52: "Knowing he or she won't be forgotten and will still be loved, talked to, and visited even after death," item 54: "Play therapy focused on illness-related topics," item 56: "Alternative therapies such as art and music," item 59: "People, things, activities that make the child smile and laugh," and item 70: "Ability to share with children having same illness in a safe, encouraging environment." Additionally, two new needs were also met with 100% satisfaction: "Mention/explanation of hospice care," and "Dignity."

Five needs, 4 of which were newly identified needs not in the original NAS list, remained unmet. These included: item 57: "Access to a child-friendly website for information, chats, etc.," "Preparation for all symptoms/side effects of disease," "To be believed by healthcare professionals when telling them something is wrong (trust)," "A liaison between doctors, nurses, and child," and "Consistent discipline." In addition, the summary statistic was not applicable for two needs that failed to be identified in any cases: item 46: "Child life intervention in the home," and item 65: "Confidentiality".

Research Objective 4

The fourth research objective was to assess the content validity of an empirically derived concept map of children's needs. This objective was evaluated by computing the frequencies and proportions of needs identified and needs met at the cluster level. The original seven clusters identified by Donnelly, Huff, Lindsey, and Schumacher (2003) were 1) Pain, 2) Decision Making, 3) Medical System Access and Quality, 4) Dignity and Respect, 5) Family-Oriented Care, 6) Spiritual Support, and7) Psychosocial Support.

In Table 5, summary statistics for the needs clusters are presented. Note that the number of items varies by cluster, from a low of 3 in the pain cluster to 23 in the psychosocial needs cluster. The number of items sets an upper limit in terms of the number of needs that can be identified; thus direct comparisons across clusters will not be made. Overall, however, it is apparent that on average, at least one need per cluster was typical in these cases. The highest proportions of needs satisfied were spiritual (.87), psychosocial (.83) and dignity/respect (.84). It is encouraging that medical system access and quality needs were met in 83% of the cases. Less encouraging was that pain needs were met at the lowest rate in this set of cases at .66 needs.

Six new needs, not included in the original 74, were identified. No new Pain, Decision Making, or Spiritual needs were apparent. New needs classifiable under cluster 3, Medical System Access and Quality included "Mention/explanation of hospice care," "To be believed by healthcare professionals when telling them something is wrong (trust)," and "A liaison between doctors, nurses, and the child." Clearly, the need for "Dignity" would be classified under cluster 4, while the need for "Consistent Discipline" could be added to the cluster 5, which represents Family-Oriented Needs. The final newly identified need, "Preparation for all symptoms/side effects of the disease" would best fit in cluster 7, representing Psychosocial Support.

Chapter Summary

An evaluation of this study's research objectives yielded various results. First, many of the needs identified were included in the original 74 needs of the NAS, however, 6 additional needs were also identified. Further, 2 of the original needs failed to be identified in any of the cases included in the study. The original seven cluster model was slightly expanded by the addition of these 6 new needs, which fell in the Medical System Access and Quality, Dignity and Respect, Family-Oriented care, and Psychosocial Support cluster areas.

Evidence of differential need identification and satisfaction across sub-groups, including the child's gender, age, family-structure, and diagnosis was present. Overall, several needs ($n=21$) were met with 100% satisfaction wherever identified, though some needs ($n=7$) remained unmet in all cases in which they were identified. Despite the fact that children with malignancies evidenced nearly twice as many needs as the children without malignancies, the proportions of needs met and quality of life ratings were similar.

There was evidence that the total number of needs present in a case is much less important than the proportion of needs met in terms of quality of life. The correlation between

36

the total number of needs met and the UNISCALE score was non-significant but the correlation

between the proportion of needs met and the UNISCALE score was strong, positive and

significant ($r = .75$, $p < .001$)

CHAPTER 5

DISCUSSION

Inclusion/Exclusion Criteria

This study aimed to access the full body of extant relevant case studies, however, it must

be noted that this body of literature increases consistently, with new journal articles, books, and

personal accounts published each day. Consequently, the cases included herein may be

representative of the full body of extant case literature on seriously and terminally ill-children at

the time of the analysis, but are limited by time and language. Because several books and

personal stories have likely been published since the inception of this analysis, it seems more

reasonable that the included cases offer a representative sample of the population, with differing

needs, diagnoses, and outcomes.

Case Studies

Forty-nine individual cases were identified and considered appropriate for inclusion in

the study. Some variation in age was noted, with 5 children falling in the infant only range, the

majority of children, eighteen, in the child only range, and 7 children falling in the teen only

range. Additionally, 11 children ranged in age from infancy through childhood, 4 children were

in the childhood through teenage range, and 3 children fell in the infancy through teenage age

range. The relatively small number of infantile cases observed is likely secondary to the

inclusion requirement that studies be longitudinal. Race and ethnicity were examined, but failed

to be identified in such a high number of cases ($n=34$) that any data regarding this demographic

variable were not complete enough to be evaluated.

Children in the cases experienced a number of different illnesses, the most prevalent of

which was some form of malignancy, or, cancer ($n=21$). The second most frequently observed diagnosis was cystic fibrosis (CF) ($n=11$), due in large part to Bluebond-Langner's (1996) book that focused specifically on 10 children from this population. Other diagnoses included, but were not limited to: Type I Diabetes, Zellweger Syndrome, Multiple Sultafase Deficiency, and Sturge-Weber Syndrome.

Children living with both parents were represented in a significant majority of the cases ($n=42$). Children living with only their mother were represented in only three of the cases, while children living in "other" living situations, such as foster care or with grandparents, constituted just four of the cases. Given the current belief that traditional, two-parent families are the exception, rather than the norm in modern society, the cases included in this study may not be representative of today's typical families.

Additional caution should be noted regarding the body of literature from which the cases included in the study were drawn. It is, no doubt, a difficult decision to share the intimate details of a child's illness, and one might contend that those parents, children, and healthcare professionals who do choose to share their stories are outside of the "normal" realm of social boundaries. Possibly, the cases that are published or communicated otherwise are those in which the child experienced considerable difficulty or ease coping and persevering.

The Coding Procedures

The Needs Assessment Survey (NAS) is a recently designed instrument. Indeed, one of the goals of the present study was to examine the content validity of the concept map that was the basis of the coding scheme employed. In order to maximize reliability, consensus coding was utilized, with two independent trained raters coding each of the 49 cases. With the addition of the newly identified six needs, and increased confidence that the original 74 needs should be retained, future research may focus on examination of reliability of the coding scheme as well as internal consistency reliability of the items and clusters.

Method

Although case synthesis is not new, it is a methodology with roots in disciplines other than the social sciences (i.e., business). While the case synthesis method and aggregation of archival data may be a common practice in other fields of study, it is improbable that a case analysis of the type undertaken herein has been attempted previously. Because the coding schemes are generally concise and succinct, meta-analytic study is often used in the social sciences as a well-regarded methodology. Case analysis, and further, case synthesis, allows for the extrapolation of very detailed information, providing the researcher with predominantly qualitative data. Quantitative data in the form of descriptive statistics can also be provided through case the case analysis method.

Evaluation of the Previous Model

The Needs Assessment Survey began with an Internet survey of 50 healthcare practitioners, program administrators, and policy makers familiar with the care of seriously and terminally ill children and their families. The original 74 needs were considered to be the palliative care needs of children at the end-of-life. Of the 49 cases studied, however, only 8 children accessed formal palliative care services, while an additional 10 cases included children and families that received hospice care. To clarify, palliative care is similar to hospice care in that the focus is comfort rather than curative care. This case synthesis provides support for continuing study of many of the original 74 needs, but also uncovered important areas of need not previously identified. In order to provide a definitive and comparable comparison of the fit of the seven-cluster model, a replication of the concept mapping analysis and sorting method used in the original concept mapping study with the children in the current study would be necessary. Due to the fact that the data herein are archival, an exact replication is not viable, however a similar study with children currently experiencing serious illness is recommended.

Need Assessment, Satisfaction, and Outcome

The study results reveal that all children in the included cases have needs that were originally identified on the NAS. Some families did, however, also indicate needs that were not included on the original list of 74 items. Most noteworthy, the top 3 needs identified, were also the top 3 needs that were met – item 15: "Opportunities to be cared for by loving family," item 20: "Fun," and item 43: "Love". Of note is the fact that although the Perrin et al. (2000) study indicated that the need for information was most frequently noted by parents as not being met adequately, this need was not identified in any of the cases studied. It is possible that this need overlaps with one of the original 74 needs, and therefore was not identified as a unique need. It is also probable that the need for information is most salient in the diagnosis stage, rather than throughout the course of the illness, and was not recognized as a need in the cases studied because a large number of the cases reported on the illness after diagnosis.

The proportions of needs met vs. identified seem to be indicative of an agreement between what children need and what services and support they received, although simple frequencies and proportions fail to assess the importance of needs. Although some needs may be identified and met more frequently than others, these are not necessarily the most critical needs of the child. However, given the significant correlation between the overall number of needs met, and the overall UNISCALE scores, it can be inferred that children who have a higher number of their needs met are also functioning at a higher level (UNISCALE score). It is also possible that these children with higher UNISCALE scores may have been functioning at a higher level prior to their diagnosis and subsequent illness. The importance of a standardized assessment tool to measure needs is imperative, however, given the significant relationship between needs satisfaction and general quality of life, as measured by the modified UNISCALE. Individualized, ongoing treatment planning based on standardized assessment of needs would potentially be the foundation for clinical trials of various specific interventions related to those needs. Pending finalization of a standard needs assessment, hypothesis testing based on such needs assessments, as has been followed successfully in the adult palliative care and hospice environments, is considered valuable future research (Emanuel, Alpert & Emanuel, 2001).

Implications for Clinical Practice and Further Research

Children are different, and experience different needs throughout their lives. This is especially true when a child is experiencing a serious or life-threatening illness. Given the findings herein, it is crucial that needs are assessed continuously, from diagnosis through the end-of-life. As the child continues to age, and the disease continues to progress, it is highly likely that the child's needs will change; if these needs are to be met satisfactorily, they need to be assessed in an ongoing fashion. As mentioned previously, needs that may be identified frequently may not be the most critical needs of the child and family. It may simply be that the needs most frequently identified are those that are most common, or most easily met by healthcare professionals and/or the child's family. An example is the need for "Love" which was both identified and met with high frequency. It is plausible, however, to presume that parents who are willing to share their child's story are those who demonstrate love for their child.

Though there are several needs that were identified frequently across age, diagnosis, gender, and family structure, there are also needs that were identified more commonly in one group or another. Different assessment tools may, indeed, prove beneficial to the child in terms

42

of assessing key issues in specific populations, however, many of these groups have overlapping characteristics. Additionally, needs assessment tools designed for specific populations may omit salient needs that are atypical for a particular group. The question arises, then, of how many needs must go unsatisfied before overall quality of life and functioning begin to decline? An attempt to answer this question warrants further investigation. Case study research, though valuable and practical for our purposes, is probably not the most effective means of answering this question; rather, research with live subjects would allow for more generalizable results. The NAS, while not a complete instrument, may be best utilized if administered during a structured interview, which would allow for clarification and elaboration of needs identified by the child participant.

Pediatric palliative care and hospice care for children are in their infancy at this time. In order to improve the outcome of such care, it is essential that we first understand the needs of those receiving care. The current study is a first attempt at enumerating and evaluating the needs of seriously and terminally-ill children through case analysis and synthesis.

References

Bessell, A.G. (2001). Children surviving cancer: Psychosocial adjustment, quality of life, and
school experiences. *Exceptional Children, 67,* 345-359.

Bluebond-Langner, M. (1978). *The Private Worlds of Dying Children,* New York: Princeton.

*Bluebond-Langner, M. (1996). *In the shadow of illness: Parents and siblings of the
chronically ill child.* Princeton, NJ: Princeton University Press.

*Bowden, L. (2002). *Magical story: A teenager's inspiring battle with Hodgkin's
disease.* Lancaster, OH: Lucky Press.

*Buckingham, R. W. (1983). *A special kind of love: Care of the dying child.* New York:
Continuum Press.

*Buff, D. (2000). A precious gift from my dying son. *Medical Economics, 77,*
71-72, 77-78.

*Campbell, T. (1998). Caring for a technology dependent child: A case study. *Nursing
Praxis in New Zealand, 13,* 5-10.

*Carley, L. (1986). The family loved Sammy but hated each other. *Nursing, 16,* 44-
46.

*Carroll, M. L., & Griffin, R. (1997). Reframing life's puzzle: Support for the bereaved
child. *American Journal of Hospice and Palliative Care, 14,* 231-235.

*Clayton, M. F. (1996). Caring for Carl at home. *Home Healthcare Nurse, 14,* 605-
608.

Creswell, J.W. (1998). Qualitative Inquiry and Research Design: Choosing Among the Five
Traditions, Thousand Oaks, CA: Sage.

*Deford, F. (1997). *Alex: The life of a child.* Nashville, TN: Rutledge Hill Press.

*Dietrich, T., & Dietrich, D. (2000). *The spirit of Lo: An ordinary family's extraordinary journey.* Tulsa, OK: Mind Matters Inc.

Donnelly, J.P., Huff, S.M., Lindsey, M.L., McMahon, K. & Schumacher, J.D. (in press, 2005). *The needs of children with life limiting conditions: A healthcare provider-based model.* American Journal of Hospice & Palliative Medicine.

Donnelly, J.P., Huff, S.H., Lindsey, M.L., & Schumacher, J.D. (2003). Progress in Pediatric Palliative Care in New York State: A Demonstration Project. In M. Field & R. Behrman (Eds.) *When Children Die: Improving Palliative and End-of-Life Care for Children and Their Families.* 638-664. Washington, DC: National Academies Press.

*Ekwerike, D. O. (1999). A case study of the impact of sickle cell disease on the educational experience and psychosocial wellness of a school age child. *Dissertation Abstracts International Section A: Humanities & Social Sciences, 60*(3A), 0893. (UMI No. 9923547).

Emanuel, L.L., Alpert, H.R. & Emanuel, E.E. (2001). Concise screening questions for clinical assessments of terminal care: The needs near the end-of-life care screening tool. *Journal of Palliative Medicine,4,* 465-474.

Feudtner, C., Christakis, D., Zimmerman, F., Muldoon, J., Neff, J. & Koepsell, T. (2002). Characteristics of deaths occurring in children's hospitals: Implications for supportive care services. *Pediatrics, 109,* 887-893.

Feudtner, C., Hays, R., Haynes, G., Geyer, R., Neff, J., & Koepsell, T. D. (2001). Deaths attributed to pediatric complex chronic conditions: National trends and implications for supportive care. *Pediatrics, 107*(6).

*Gallo, A. M. (1991). Family adaptation in childhood chronic illness: A case report. *Journal of Pediatric Health Care, 5,* 78-85.

*Gino, C. (1997). Only a father. *Nursing, 27,* 43-45.

*Gray, S. (2004). Retrieved February 12, 2004. Journal posted to Caringbridge, archived at http://www.caringbridge.org/nj/samigray/history.htm

*Grealy, L. (1994). *Autobiography of a face.* Boston: Houghton Mifflin Company.

*Higgins-Brunner, S. (1996). *Perfect vision.* Fuquay-Varina, VA: Research Triangle Publishing Inc.

*Hilderly, L. J., Iwamoto, R. R., & Knobf, M. T. (2002). Pain and suffering in an adolescent with neuroblastoma. *Cancer Practice, 10,* 54-58.

*Housden, M. (2002). *Hannah's gift: Lessons from a life fully lived.* New York: Bantam Books.

*Irwin, C. (1996). Samantha's wish. *Nursing Times, 92,* 30-31.

*Jennings, L. G. (1999). Jose. *Home Care Provider, 4,* 218-219.

Jensen, J.L. & Rodgers, R. (2001). Cumulating the intellectual gold of case study research. *Public Administration Review, 61,* 236-46.

Joy, R. (2001). Satisfying human needs. *World Tobacco, July,* 13-14.

*Kernan-Bowie, W. (1977). Story of a first born. *Omega, 8,* 1-17.

*Knoop, T., Murphy, P., Rundlett, C., Hubbard, F., Hicks, C., Stedman, P., Cherry, G., Laubach, H., & Hall, J. (1995). Simply supporting Sarah. *Nursing, 25,* 48-53.

Kiel, J.M. (1999). Reshaping Maslow's Hierarchy of Needs to reflect today's educational and managerial philosophies. *Journal of Instructional Psychology, 26,* 167.

*Lawler, M. K. (1977). An adolescent's behavioral responses to a second renal transplant. *Maternal-Child Nursing Journal, 6,* 51-63.

*Lister, E. (2001). Liza's death: A personal recollection. *Journal of Pain and Symptom Management, 21,* 243-249.

Loftquist, L. & Dawis, R. (1984). *A Psychological Theory of Work Adjustment,* Minneapolis, MN: University of Minnesota Press.

*Lyon, M. E., Townsend-Akpan, C, & Thompson, A. (2001). Spirituality and end-of-life care for an adolescent with AIDS. *AIDS Patient Care and STDs, 15,* 555-560.

Madan-Swain, A., Sexson, S.B., Brown, R.T. & Ragab, A. (1993). Family adaptation and coping among siblings of cancer patients, their brothers and sisters, and non-clinical controls. *The American Journal of Family Therapy, 21,* 60-70.

McHale, J. & McHale M.C. (1979). Meeting basic human needs. *Annals of the American Academy of Political and Social Science, 442,* 13-27.

*Meagher, D. K., & Taner Leff, P. (1989). In Marie's memory: The rights of a child with life-threatening or terminal illness. *Omega, 20,* 177-191.

*Mizen-McCarthy, S., & Gallo, A. M. (1992). A case illustration of family management style. *Journal of Pediatric Nursing, 7,* 395-402.

Newacheck, P.W., Hughes, D., Hung, Y., Wong, S. & Stoddard, J. (2000). The unmet health needs of America's children. *Pediatrics, 104,* 989-997.

O'Halloran, C.M. & Altmaier, E.M. (1996). Awareness of death among children: Does a life-threatening illness alter the process of discovery? *Journal of Counseling & Development, 74,* 259-262.

Parker, V.G. & Logan, B.N. (2000). Students', parents', and teachers' perceptions of health needs of school-age children: Implications for nurse practitioners. *Family and Community Health, 23,* 62-68.

Perrin, E.C., Lewkowicz, C. & Young, M.H. (2000). Shared vision: Concordance among fathers, mothers, and pediatricians about unmet needs of children with chronic health conditions. *Pediatrics,* 105, 277-285.

*Ramer-Chrastek, J. (2000). Hospice care for a terminally-ill child in the school setting. *Journal of School Nursing, 16,* 52-56.

Randolph, L. (1994). Our children's health. *Social Policy, Summer,* 25-30.

*Sandoval, N. (2003). Retrieved February 12, 2004. Journal posted to Caringbridge, archived at http://www.caringbridge.org/id/ntsandoval/history.htm

*Schrauger, B. (2001). *Walking Taylor home.* Nashville, TN: W Publishing Group.

*Scott, T. E. (1996). Daniel. *Journal of Pediatric Oncology Nursing, 13,* 56-57.

*Showalter, S. E. (1997). Now I lay me down to sleep. Remembering Walter: A child preparing to die. *American Journal of Hospice and Palliative Care, 14,* 239-243.

*Stephenson, D. (1994). Portrait of a creatively gifted child facing cancer. *Creativity Research, 7,* 71-77.

*Swanson, T. (2004). Mighty like a rose. *Pediatric Rehabilitation, 7,* 221-223.

*Walker, M. B., Hilbert, G. A., & Rinehart, J. (1999). Face to face with Sturge-Weber syndrome. *Journal of the Society of Pediatric Nurses, 4,* 74-82.

Wallinga, C. & Skeen, P. (1996). Siblings of hospitalized and ill children: The teacher's role in helping these forgotten family members. *Young Children, 51(6),* 78-83.

Wildrick, D., Parker-Fisher, S. & Morales, A. (1996). Quality of life in children with well-controlled Epilepsy. *Journal of Neuroscience Nursing, 28(3),* 192-198.

*Wolfe, J. J. (1997). Hospice support for families facing multiple deaths of children. *American Journal of Hospice and Palliative Care, 14,* 224-227.

*Wolford, C. B., & Wolford, F. (1999). *My story about cancer.* Santa Ana, CA: Seven Locks Press.

*Wren, S. (n.d.). *Jazzy Wren: My battle with a medulloblastoma brain tumor.* Retrieved February 12, 2004, from http://www.home.aone.net.au/wren/jazmin.htm

Zemke, R. (1998). Maslow for a new millenium. *Training, 35,* 54-59.

Table 1

Overall Frequencies and Proportions of Individual Needs

Need	f	Proportion of Cases (N=49)
15. Opportunities to be cared for by loving family	31	.63
20. Fun	25	.51
43. Love	25	.51
11. Talk about feelings and fears	23	.47
47. Competent pediatric-trained professionals	23	.47
5. Developmentally appropriate activities and information	22	.45
9. To be clearly valued as an individual by having preferences solicited and acted upon to the extent reasonable	22	.45
28. Effective pain management	22	.45
59. People, things, activities that make the child smile & laugh	22	.45
27. Pleasant distractions from the situation	21	.43
3. Honesty	20	.41
12. Compassionate care (non-judgmental love, touch, etc.)	20	.41
66. To have the critical nature of the illness and possibility acknowledged	20	.41
30. Stimulation (via school activity, play, family activities, etc.)	19	.39
35. To be physically touched and soothed	19	.39
37. Parents who are receiving sufficient support so that they can focus on the child and siblings as much as possible	19	.39
34. Access to peers	18	.37
60. Comfort	18	.37
71. Continuity of "Normal Life" within their family, school, faith/social community and circle of friends	18	.37
7. To address fears with a competent professional	17	.35

Need	f	Proportion
36. To acknowledge the sadness of the child and those who love him or her about the illness and possibility of death	17	.35
67. Regular contact with peers	17	.35
69. Accurate assessment and effective treatment of pain and non-pain symptoms	17	.35
4. Laughter for release	16	.33
10. Comforting atmosphere with pain control	16	.33
21. Sense of control over life or some aspects of it	16	.33
49. As much time at home as possible	16	.33
14. Clear, developmentally appropriate explanations of care options, benefits, and burdens	15	.31
51. The right to say no	15	.31
61. Nutritional support in the home	15	.31
63. Parents who are mentally healthy and functional under stress	15	.31
70. Ability to share with other children having same illness in a safe, encouraging environment	15	.31
73. To have a say in the treatment plan	15	.31
19. Unlimited access to family, as desired by child	14	.29
32. Quality of life	14	.29
55. Assessment of concerns around meaning, loss and spiritual issues and effective means of addressing these (existential issues)	13	.27
6. Consistency in professional caregivers throughout the illness, including the end-stage	12	.25
26. Prayers	12	.25

Need	f	Proportion
31. Consistent pain assessment	12	.25
45. Focus on the child's hopes and dreams, including assistance when their hopes and dreams will likely not be met	11	.22
50. Networking with other children experiencing similar illness, treatment, etc.	11	.22
72. Help with the visual part of the illness so that the child feels as good as possible about his or her body and appearance	11	.22
53. Family-focused care	10	.20
33. Flexibility to receive care wherever it is safe	9	.18
40. The ability to transition in or out of the hospital as needed	8	.16
2. Coordinated healthcare provided in a timely, convenient and pleasant environment	7	.14
13. Assessment of preferences and goals for social interaction and facilitation of those preferences and goals	7	.14
16. Assessment of perceptions of burdens and benefits of care	7	.14
22. Self-relaxation skills	7	.14
39. Privacy	7	.14
41. Spirituality in their care	7	.14
56. Alternative therapies such as art and music	7	.14
58. To feel that the child has not caused many other losses for the family (e.g., financial struggles)	7	.14
48. Assessment of personal goals of care	6	.12
68. Being able to remain in familiar surroundings with familiar people	6	.12
8. Not spending hours and hours in clinics and waiting rooms	4	.08
24. To be reassured that he or she is important and will be remembered	4	.08

Need	f	Proportion
29. To maintain a sense of self	4	.08
64. To create a personal legacy	4	.08
1. Access to palliative care benefit from the time of diagnosis without a time constraint (such as the hospice regulation)	3	.06
23. Culturally sensitive care	3	.06
25. Understandable information about supportive and palliative and hospice care to reduce anxiety and unknowns	3	.06
38. Ability for NP/MDs to make home visits	3	.06
42. Nurses/HHAs who are trained in pediatrics	3	.06
52. Knowing he or she won't be forgotten and will still be loved, talked to and visited even after death	3	.06
17. Translators if the child's first language is not English	2	.04
44. Peer support groups	2	.04
54. Play therapy that focuses on illness-related topics	2	.04
62. Care for the healthcare provider so that they can care for the children in a more caring and nurturing way	2	.04
74. Reduction of barriers imposed by the 6-month limit of the hospice benefit	2	.04
18. Being able to give home blood transfusions, especially platelets so the child does not bleed out at home	1	.02
57. Access to a child-friendly website for information, chats, etc.	1	.02
+ Mention/explanation of hospice care	1	.02
+ Preparation for all symptoms/side effects of disease	1	.02
+ To be believed by healthcare professionals when telling them something is wrong (trust)	1	.02
+ A liaison between doctors, nurses, and the child	1	.02

Need	f	Proportion
+ Dignity	1	.02
+ Consistent discipline	1	.02
46. Child life intervention in the home	0	.00
65. Confidentiality	0	.00

Table 2

Overall Frequencies and Proportions of Need Satisfaction

Need	f	Proportion
15. Opportunities to be cared for by loving family	27	.55
20. Fun	25	.51
43. Love	24	.49
59. People, things, activities that make the child smile & laugh	22	.45
27. Pleasant distractions from the situation	21	.43
5. Developmentally appropriate activities and information	19	.39
9. To be clearly valued as an individual by having preferences solicited and acted upon, to the extent reasonable	19	.39
11. To talk about their feelings and fears	19	.39
12. Compassionate care (nonjudgmental love, touch, long talks, looking out of a window, feeling the sun)	18	.37
35. To be physically touched and soothed	18	.37
30. Stimulation (via school activity, play, family activities, etc.)	17	.35
4. Laughter for release	16	.33
66. To have the critical nature of the illness and possibility of death acknowledged	16	.33
3. Honesty	15	.31
28. Effective pain management	15	.31
51. The right to say no	15	.31
70. Ability to share with children having same illness in a safe and encouraging environment	15	.31
10. Comforting atmosphere with pain control	14	.29
21. Sense of control over life or some aspects of it	14	.29
34. Access to peers	14	.29

Need	f	Proportion
36. To acknowledge the sadness of the child and those who love him or her about the illness and possibility of death	14	.29
60. Comfort	14	.29
73. To have a say in the treatment plan	14	.29
7. To address fears with a competent professional	13	.27
47. Competent pediatric-trained professional caregivers	13	.27
61. Nutritional support in the home	13	.27
67. Regular contact with peers	13	.27
19. Unlimited access to family, as desired by child	12	.25
26. Prayers	12	.25
32. Quality of life	12	.25
49. As much time at home as possible	12	.25
14. Clear, developmentally appropriate explanations of care benefits and burdens	11	.22
50. Networking with other children experiencing a similar illness, treatment, etc.	11	.22
71. Continuity of "Normal Life" within their family, school, faith/social community and circle of friends	11	.22
31. Consistent pain assessment	10	.20
37. Parents who are receiving sufficient support so that they can focus on the child and siblings as much as possible	10	.20
55. Assessment of concerns around meaning, loss and spiritual issues, and effective means of addressing these (existential issues)	10	.20
45. Focus on the child's hopes and dreams, including assistance when their hopes and dreams will likely not be met	9	.18
53. Family-focused care	9	.18

Need	f	Proportion
33. Flexibility to receive care wherever it is safe	8	.16
40. The ability to transition in or out of the hospital as needed	8	.16
69. Accurate assessment and effective treatment of pain and non-pain symptoms	8	.16
6. Consistency in professional caregivers throughout the illness, including the end-stage	7	.14
13. Assessment of preferences and goals for social interaction and facilitation of those preferences and goals	7	.14
56. Alternative therapies such as art and music	7	.14
39. Privacy	6	.12
41. Spirituality in their care	6	.12
63. Parents who are mentally healthy and functional under stress	6	.12
2. Coordinated healthcare provided in a timely, convenient, and pleasant environment	5	.10
68. Being able to remain in familiar surroundings with familiar people	5	.10
24. To be reassured that he or she is important and will be remembered	4	.08
58. To not feel that the child has caused many other losses for the family (e.g., financial struggles)	4	.08
72. Help with the visual part of the illness so that the child feels as good as possible about his or her body and appearance	4	.08
16. Assessment of perceptions of burdens and benefits of care	3	.06
22. Self-relaxation skills	3	.06
23. Culturally-sensitive care	3	.06
29. To maintain a sense of self	3	.06
38. Ability for NP/MDs to make home visits	3	.06
48. Assessment of personal goals of care	3	.06

Need	f	Proportion
52. Knowing he or she won't be forgotten and will still be loved, talked to, and visited even after death	3	.06
64. To create a personal legacy	3	.06
17. Translators if the child's first language is not English	2	.04
42. Nurses/HHAs who are trained in pediatrics	2	.04
44. Peer support groups	2	.04
54. Play therapy that focuses on illness-related topics	2	.04
1. Access to palliative care benefits from the time of diagnosis without a time constraint (such as the hospice regulation)	1	.02
8. Not spending hours and hours in clinics and waiting rooms	1	.02
18. Being able to give home blood transfusions, especially platelets so the child does not bleed out at home	1	.02
25. Understandable information about supportive and palliative and hospice care to reduce anxiety and unknowns	1	.02
62. Care for healthcare providers so that they can care for the children in a more caring and nurturing way	1	.02
74. Reduction of barriers imposed by the 6-month limit of the hospice benefit	1	.02
+ Mention/explanation of hospice care	1	.02
+ Dignity	1	.02
46. Child life intervention in the home	0	.00
57. Access to a child-friendly website for information, chats, etc.	0	.00
65. Confidentiality	0	.00
+ Preparation for all symptoms/side effects of disease	0	.00
+ To be believed by healthcare professionals when telling them something is wrong	0	.00

Need	f	Proportion
+ A liaison between doctors, nurses, and the child	0	.00
+ Consistent discipline	0	.00

Table 3

Overall UNISCALE Frequencies and Percentages

UNISCALE Score	f	Percent	Valid Percent
1	1	2.0	3.4
2	2	4.1	6.9
3	2	4.1	6.9
4	3	6.1	10.3
5	2	4.1	6.9
6	1	2.0	3.4
7	3	6.1	10.3
8	6	12.2	20.7
9	6	12.2	20.7
10	3	6.1	10.3
Total	29	59.2	100.0
Missing	20	40.8	
Total	49	100.0	

Table 4

*Proportion of **Identified** Needs Met*

Need	Proportion
4. Laughter for release	1.00
13. Assessment of preferences & goals for social interaction and facilitation of those preferences & goals	1.00
17. Translators if the child's first language is not English	1.00
18. Being able to give home blood transfusions, especially platelets so the child does not bleed out at home	1.00
20. Fun	1.00
23. Culturally-sensitive care	1.00
24. To be reassured that he or she is important and will be remembered	1.00
26. Prayers	1.00
27. Pleasant distractions from the situation	1.00
38. Ability for NP/MDs to make home visits	1.00
40. The ability to transition in or out of the hospital as needed	1.00
44. Peer support groups	1.00
50. Networking with other children experiencing a similar illness, treatment, etc.	1.00
51. The right to say no	1.00
52. Knowing he or she won't be forgotten and will still be loved, talked to, and visited even after death	1.00
54. Play therapy that focuses on illness-related topics	1.00
56. Alternative therapies such as art and music	1.00
59. People, things, activities that make the child smile and laugh	1.00
70. Ability to share with children having same illness in a safe, encouraging environment	1.00
+ Mention/explanation of hospice care	1.00

Need	Proportion
+ Dignity	1.00
43. Love	.96
35. To be physically touched and soothed (e.g. massage)	.95
73. To have a say in the treatment plan	.93
12. Compassionate care (non-judgmental love, touch, long talks, etc.)	.90
53. Family-focused care	.90
30. Stimulation (via school activity, play, family activities, etc.)	.89
33. Flexibility to receive care wherever it is safe	.89
10. Comforting atmosphere with pain control	.88
21. Sense of control over life or some aspects of it	.88
15. Opportunities to be cared for by loving family	.87
61. Nutritional support in the home	.87
5. Developmentally appropriate activities & information	.86
9. To be clearly valued as an individual by having preferences solicited and acted upon to the extent reasonable	.86
19. Unlimited access to family, as desired by child	.86
32. Quality of life	.86
39. Privacy	.86
41. Spirituality in their care	.86
11. Talk about their feelings and fears	.83
31. Consistent pain assessment	.83
68. Being able to remain in familiar surroundings with familiar people	.83
36. To acknowledge the sadness of the child and those who love him or her about the illness and possibility of death	.82
45. Focus on the child's hopes and dreams, including assistance when those hopes and dreams will likely not be met	.82

Need	Proportion
66. To have the critical nature of the illness and possibility of death acknowledged	.80
34. Access to peers	.78
60. Comforting atmosphere with pain control	.78
55. Assessment of concerns around meaning, loss, and spiritual issues and effective means of addressing these (existential issues)	.77
7. To address fears with a competent professional	.76
67. Regular contact with peers	.76
3. Honesty	.75
29. To maintain a sense of self	.75
49. As much time at home as possible (and as little time in the hospital)	.75
64. To create a personal legacy	.75
14. Clear, developmentally appropriate explanations of care options, benefits, and burdens	.73
2. Coordinated healthcare provided in a timely, convenient, and pleasant environment	.71
28. Effective pain management	.68
42. Nurses/HHAs who are trained in pediatrics	.67
71. Continuity of "Normal Life" within family, school, faith/social community and circle of friends	.61
6. Consistency in professional caregivers throughout the illness, including the end-stage	.58
47. Competent pediatric-trained professional caregivers	.57
58. To not feel that the child has caused many other losses for the family (e.g. financial struggles)	.57
37. Parents who are receiving sufficient support so they can focus on the child and siblings as much as possible	.53

Need	Proportion
48. Assessment of personal goals of care	.50
62. Care for the healthcare provider so that they can care for the children in a more caring and nurturing way	.50
74. Reduction of barriers imposed by the 6 month limit of the hospice benefit	.50
69. Accurate assessment and effective treatment of pain and non-pain symptoms	.47
16. Assessment of perceptions of burdens and benefits of care	.43
22. Self-relaxation skills	.43
63. Parents who are mentally healthy and functional under stress	.40
72. Help with the visual part of the illness so that the child feels as good as possible about his or her body and appearance	.36
1. Access to palliative care benefit from the time of diagnosis without a time constraint (such as the hospice regulation)	.33
25. Understandable information about supportive and palliative and hospice care to reduce anxiety and unknowns	.33
8. Not spending hours and hours in clinics and waiting rooms	.25
57. Access to a child-friendly website for information, chats, etc.	.00
+ Preparation for all symptoms/side effects of disease	.00
+ To be believed by healthcare professionals when telling them something is wrong	.00
+ A liaison between doctors, nurses, and child	.00
+ Consistent discipline	.00
46. Child life intervention in the home	*
65. Confidentiality	*

Note: Maximum possible frequency = 49
+ indicates a newly identified need, not included in the original 74 on the NAS
  • indicates a need that was not identified in any cases, and therefore, remained unmet

Table 5

Means and Proportions of Needs Identified and Needs Met by Age

Age	Mean Needs Identified	Mean Needs Met	Proportion	Mean UNISCALE
Infant Only	9.2 (12.83)	7.8 (11.97)	.78 (.31)	4.50 (4.95)
Child Only	20.06 (12.47)	17.78 (12.47)	.86 (.18)	7.11 (2.67)
Teen/Adolescent Only	20.29 (10.73)	18.57 (9.54)	.93 (.08)	6.50 (2.38)
Infant – Child	17.09 (11.41)	12.73 (10.22)	.74 (.24)	7.33 (2.73)
Child – Teen/ Adolescent	22.50 (13.77)	12.00 (2.45)	.55 (3.12)	5.50 (3.12)
Infant – Teen/ Adolescent	11.33 (5.13)	5.33 (3.21)	.55 (.36)	6.33 (3.22)

Table 6

Descriptive Statistics for Needs Identified, Needs Met, and Proportion Met by Cluster

Variable & # Items per Cluster	Needs Identified	Needs Met	Proportion Met
	M (SD)	*M (SD)*	*M (SD)*
Pain (3)	1.04 (1.14)	.67 (1.01)	.66 (.46)
Decision Making (6)	.98 (1.31)	.69 (1.10)	.72 (.43)
Medical System Access & Quality (12)	1.98 (1.80)	1.41 (1.57)	.83 (.29)
Dignity/Respect (14)	3.61 (2.94)	3.00 (2.68)	.84 (.29)
Family-oriented Care (7)	1.06 (1.21)	.90 (1.19)	.77 (.39)
Spiritual (9)	1.89 (2.23)	1.67 (2.06)	.87 (.28)
Psychosocial (23)	7.50 (4.80)	6.12 (4.42)	.83 (.26)

Appendix A

Coding Sheet for Case Studies, including the Needs Assessment Survey

Case Synthesis Coding Sheet

Case Information

Case Identification #:_____

Case reporter (name & relationship to child):_____

Citation:_____

Child Information
Age(s)
      1. At Diagnosis   _____
      2. At Death   _____
      3. At Case Report _____

Gender
      ❏ Male
      ❏ Female
      ❏ Unknown

Diagnosis & Staging Information
    Type of Complex Chronic Conditions
    List co-morbidities to the right of the category into which they best fit.
  ❏ Neuromuscular
      ❏ Brain and spinal cord malformations
      ❏ Mental retardation
      ❏ Central nervous system degeneration and disease
      ❏ Infantile cerebral palsy
      ❏ Epilepsy
      ❏ Muscular dystrophies and myopathies
  ❏ Cardiovascular
      ❏ Heart and great vessel malformations
      ❏ Cardiomyopathies
      ❏ Conduction disorders and dysrhytmias
  ❏ Respiratory
      ❏ Respiratory malformations
      ❏ Chronic respiratory disease
      ❏ Cystic fibrosis
  ❏ Renal
      ❏ Congenital nomalies
      ❏ Chronic renal failure
  ❏ Gastrointestinal
      ❏ Congenital anomalies
      ❏ Chronic liver disease and cirrhosis
      ❏ Inflammatory bowel disease
  ❏ Hematology and Immunodeficiency
      ❏ Sickle cell disease

- ❑ Hereditary anemias
- ❑ Hereditary immunodeficiency
- ❑ Human immunodeficiency virus disease

❑ Metabolic
- ❑ Amino acid metabolism
- ❑ Carbohydrate metabolism
- ❑ Lipid metabolism
- ❑ Storage disorders
- ❑ Other metabolic disorders _____

❑ Other Congenital or Genetic Defect
- ❑ Chromosomal anomalies
- ❑ Bone and joint anomalies

- ❏ Diaphragm and abdominal wall
- ❏ Other congenital anomalies _____

❏ Malignancy

Treatment
- ❏ Surgical intervention   #_____ surgeries
- ❏ Chemotherapy   #_____/_____ rounds/cycles
- ❏ Organ Transplantation   specify organ type _____
- ❏ Palliative (comfort, non-curative) Care   duration (weeks):_____
- ❏ Hospice (formal EOL program)   duration (weeks):_____
- ❏ Other   specify _____

Location at Death
- ❏ Home
- ❏ Hospital
- ❏ Other: _____

School Data
Enrollment
- ❏ Elementary School
- ❏ Middle School
- ❏ High School
- ❏ Home Schooled

Completion (last level enrolled in)
- ❏ Able to attend and complete
- ❏ Able to attend but unable to complete
- ❏ Unable to attend but complete (i.e., home-schooled/tutored)
- ❏ Unable to attend or complete

Family Data

Resides in home with:

Siblings (specify full, half, step)
Type   Age   Gender

- ❏ Mother
- ❏ Father
- ❏ Stepmother
- ❏ Stepfather
- ❏ Aunts
- ❏ Uncles
- ❏ Cousins
- ❏ Grandfather
- ❏ Grandmother
- ❏ Other: _____

Resources
- ❏ Stressed
- ❏ Adequate

Children's Needs

Identified as a need?		Identified as met?		#	STATEMENTS
Y	N	Y	N	1	Access to palliative care benefit from the time of diagnosis without a time constraint (such as the hospice regulation)
Y	N	Y	N	2	Coordinated health care provided in a timely, convenient, & pleasant environment
Y	N	Y	N	3	Honesty
Y	N	Y	N	4	Laughter for release (e.g., visiting clown programs)
Y	N	Y	N	5	Developmentally-appropriate activities & information
Y	N	Y	N	6	Consistency in professional caregivers throughout the illness, including the end-stage
Y	N	Y	N	7	To address fears with a competent professional
Y	N	Y	N	8	Not spending hours and hours in clinics and waiting rooms
Y	N	Y	N	9	To be clearly valued as an individual by having preferences solicited and acted upon, to the extent reasonable
Y	N	Y	N	10	Comforting atmosphere with pain control
Y	N	Y	N	11	Talk about their feelings and fears
Y	N	Y	N	12	Compassionate care (nonjudgmental love, touch, long talks, looking out a window, feeling the sun)
Y	N	Y	N	13	Assessment of preferences & goals for social interaction and facilitation of those preferences & goals
Y	N	Y	N	14	Clear, developmentally appropriate explanations of care options, benefits and burdens
Y	N	Y	N	15	Opportunities to be cared for by loving family
Y	N	Y	N	16	Assessment of perceptions of burdens and benefits of care
Y	N	Y	N	17	Translators if the child's first language is not English
Y	N	Y	N	18	Being able to give home blood transfusions, especially platelets so the child does not bleed out at home
Y	N	Y	N	19	Unlimited access to family, as desired by the child
Y	N	Y	N	20	Fun
Y	N	Y	N	21	Sense of control over life or some aspects of it
Y	N	Y	N	22	Self-relaxation skills
Y	N	Y	N	23	Culturally-sensitive care
Y	N	Y	N	24	To be reassured that he or she is important and will be remembered
Y	N	Y	N	25	Understandable information about supportive and palliative and hospice care to reduce anxiety and unknowns
Y	N	Y	N	26	Prayers
Y	N	Y	N	27	Pleasant distractions from the situation
Y	N	Y	N	28	Effective pain management
Y	N	Y	N	29	To maintain a sense of self
Y	N	Y	N	30	Stimulation (via school activity, play, family activities, etc.)
Y	N	Y	N	31	Consistent pain assessment
Y	N	Y	N	32	Quality of life
Y	N	Y	N	33	Flexibility to receive care wherever it is safe

Y	N	Y	N	34	Access to peers
Y	N	Y	N	35	To be physically touched and soothed (e.g., massage)
Y	N	Y	N	36	To acknowledge the sadness of the child and those who love him or her about the illness and possibility of death
Y	N	Y	N	37	Parents who are receiving sufficient support so that they can focus on the child and siblings as much as possible
Y	N	Y	N	38	Ability for NP/MD's to make home visits
Y	N	Y	N	39	Privacy
Y	N	Y	N	40	The ability to transition in or out of the hospital as needed
Y	N	Y	N	41	Spirituality in their care
Y	N	Y	N	42	Nurses/HHA's who are trained in pediatrics
Y	N	Y	N	43	Love
Y	N	Y	N	44	Peer support groups
Y	N	Y	N	45	Focus on the child's hopes and dreams, including assistance when their hopes and dreams will likely not be met
Y	N	Y	N	46	Child life intervention in the home
Y	N	Y	N	47	Competent pediatric-trained professional caregivers
Y	N	Y	N	48	Assessment of personal goals of care
Y	N	Y	N	49	As much time at home as possible (& as little time in the hospital)
Y	N	Y	N	50	Networking with other children experiencing a similar illness, treatment, etc.
Y	N	Y	N	51	The right to say no
Y	N	Y	N	52	Knowing he or she won't be forgotten and will still be loved, talked to and visited even after
Y	N	Y	N	53	Family-focused care
Y	N	Y	N	54	Play therapy that focuses on illness-related topics
Y	N	Y	N	55	Assessment of concerns around meaning, loss and spiritual issues and effective means of addressing these
Y	N	Y	N	56	Alternative therapies such as art & music
Y	N	Y	N	57	Access to a child-friendly website for information, chats, etc
Y	N	Y	N	58	To not feel that the child has caused many other losses for the family (e.g., financial struggles)
Y	N	Y	N	59	People, things, activities that make the child smile & laugh
Y	N	Y	N	60	Comfort
Y	N	Y	N	61	Nutritional support in the home
Y	N	Y	N	62	Care for the health care provider so that they can care for the children in a more caring and nurturing way
Y	N	Y	N	63	Parents who are mentally healthy and functional under stress
Y	N	Y	N	64	To create a personal legacy
Y	N	Y	N	65	Confidentiality

Y	N	Y	N	66	To have the critical nature of the illness and possibility of death acknowledged
Y	N	Y	N	67	Regular contact with peers
Y	N	Y	N	68	Being able to remain in familiar surroundings with familiar people
Y	N	Y	N	69	Accurate assessment and effective treatment of pain and non-pain symptoms
Y	N	Y	N	70	Ability to share with children having same illness in a safe, encouraging environment
Y	N	Y	N	71	Continuity of "Normal Life" within their family, school, faith/social community and circle of friends
Y	N	Y	N	72	Help with the visual part of the illness so that the child feels as good as possible about his or her body and appearance
Y	N	Y	N	73	To have a say in the treatment plan
Y	N	Y	N	74	Reduction of barriers imposed by the 6 month limit of the hospice benefit

Family's Needs

Need Ratings				STATEMENTS
Identified as a need?		Identified as met?	#	
Y	N	Y	N	1	Sensitivity to how the family makes decisions (who decides, what factors are important)
Y	N	Y	N	2	Support and understanding of the school the child attends, including the child'
Y	N	Y	N	3	Support that is tailored to the individual family situation
Y	N	Y	N	4	Competent pediatric professional caregivers
Y	N	Y	N	5	Space to release emotions and fears
Y	N	Y	N	6	Consistent effective counseling
Y	N	Y	N	7	Support for integrity of family system, inc parental relationship
Y	N	Y	N	8	Counseling & other efforts to help normalize family life
Y	N	Y	N	9	Reimbursement for physician & nurse practitioner visits at home
Y	N	Y	N	10	Respect for decisions made with regard to culture & religion
Y	N	Y	N	11	Spiritual support
Y	N	Y	N	12	Access to palliative care services in the home
Y	N	Y	N	13	Information and support in decision making
Y	N	Y	N	14	Consistent positive attention to siblings
Y	N	Y	N	15	Pastoral counseling on end-of life issues, DNRs, medical directives, etc
Y	N	Y	N	16	Support for decision making related to withdrawal of nutritional support
Y	N	Y	N	17	Advocacy and flexibility at work
Y	N	Y	N	18	Team approach to end-of-life issues
Y	N	Y	N	19	Adequate nursing
Y	N	Y	N	20	Accommodations at inpatient settings to allow family to stay nearby
Y	N	Y	N	21	Opportunities for anticipatory grieving
Y	N	Y	N	22	Clear understanding of what palliative care is
Y	N	Y	N	23	Home adaptation to make life easier for the child & family (home accessibili'
Y	N	Y	N	24	Prayers
Y	N	Y	N	25	Adequate counseling services
Y	N	Y	N	26	To be able to discuss the future with caring and competent professionals
Y	N	Y	N	27	Follow-up care after child's death, including bereavement counseling
Y	N	Y	N	28	Ways of finding hope
Y	N	Y	N	29	Help with funeral arrangements

Y	N	Y	N	30	Open lines of communication with care providers
Y	N	Y	N	31	Access to Internet in rural areas where caregivers are few and travel is difficult (Palliative Telemanagement?)
Y	N	Y	N	32	Assistance with how to tell your child where their resting place will be
Y	N	Y	N	33	To stay connected to their natural/pre-illness social circle and support system
Y	N	Y	N	34	Reimbursement for psychosocial intervention at home
Y	N	Y	N	35	Sibling support groups and information for parents on handling sibling issues
Y	N	Y	N	36	To be informed about the supportive resources within the community
Y	N	Y	N	37	Support for each family member's ways of coping with the situation
Y	N	Y	N	38	The ability to stay home with the child without financial pressure
Y	N	Y	N	39	Respite care that is reimbursed and available in the home or inpatient setting
Y	N	Y	N	40	Trained staff to provide psychosocial support to siblings
Y	N	Y	N	41	Increase in community based support systems
Y	N	Y	N	42	Ways in which family members can help ease child's pain & participate in care
Y	N	Y	N	43	Creative therapies (e.g., music, art) for those who have difficulty verbalizing their feelings
Y	N	Y	N	44	Education and/or counseling related to communication with extended family and friends
Y	N	Y	N	45	Timely accurate information about diagnosis and prognosis
Y	N	Y	N	46	Information about and assistance in connecting with important community resources
Y	N	Y	N	47	Opportunities for socialization with friends and family
Y	N	Y	N	48	Pastoral care
Y	N	Y	N	49	An advocate to coordinate services, appointments, etc
Y	N	Y	N	50	Consistency in caregivers
Y	N	Y	N	51	In-service training for school teachers & administrators on anticipatory grief, children's grief issues & how teachers can help
Y	N	Y	N	52	Childcare for siblings so parents can stay with sick child when in the hospital
Y	N	Y	N	53	Choices in care from the time of diagnosis onward
Y	N	Y	N	54	Ability to negotiate between the medical system & the family's beliefs, culture, and spiritual needs
Y	N	Y	N	55	Financial support so that parents can take time off work to spend time with their sick child & family
Y	N	Y	N	56	Information about clinical trials, especially about Phase I trials
Y	N	Y	N	57	Culturally-sensitive translators if English is not first language
Y	N	Y	N	58	Parent to parent networking
Y	N	Y	N	59	Support staff (medical & psychosocial) who are as flexible as the situation demands
Y	N	Y	N	60	Ability to continue to parent other children in the family

Y	N	Y	N	61	Support from social workers before and after death
Y	N	Y	N	62	Assistance in evaluating alternative treatments
Y	N	Y	N	63	Connections with others who have been through this to discuss what worked f (i.e., what to expect from those who "really know")

List any needs identified in this case study that are not enumerated above. For each, designate whether said need was identified as met, using Y or N.

UNISCALE Rating: _____

On a scale of 1 to 10, with 1 being the worst, and 10 being the best possible quality of life, where:

During the child's illness and treatment, overall the family experiences conditions such as:

1 = severe disruption in the family life including loss of nearly all normal roles and routines, fractured relationships within and beyond the family, maladaptive coping by more than one family member, severely strained resources, extreme emotional distress, hopelessness and helplessness, unable to find shared meaning in life

10 = successful adaptation in roles and routines to maintain family functioning, strong or even enhanced relationships with others within and beyond the family, adequate resources, realistic hopefulness, effective coping by most members of the family, able to find meaning in life.

   ☐ Insufficient Information to Discern UNISCALE rating

Did this child die a good death?   YES   NO   N/A – Child did not die

(circle one)

Consider: 1. Presence of loved ones   4. Sufficient Post-Death Care/Attention

             2. Absence of pain/symptomatology

             3. Psychological acceptance/distress

Made in the USA
Lexington, KY
30 September 2010